D1179827

From Daumier to Matisse: Selections from the John C. Whitehead Collection

From Daumier to Matisse: Selections from the John C. Whitehead Collection

ACHIM MOELLER FINE ART

Library of Congress Catalogue
Card Number: 2002103922
ISBN 0-9646052-1-x

Project Promotion by Achim Moeller
Edited by Laura Kleger
and Kathleen Howard
(Achim Moeller's foreword)
Designed by Philippe Apeloig
Print production by Paola Gribaudo
Color separation by Litho Art New, Turin
Printed by Pozzo Gros Monti,
Moncalieri, Italy

Photography credits:
Noel Allum, pp. 13, 16, 20 (right), 41, 51, 55, 59,
61, 63, 67, 71, 76, 82, 84, 86, 87, 88, 91, 93
David Hollander, 1989, p. 6
Günter Knop, 1996, pp. 14, 15, 18, 19, 20 (left), 23
(right), 25 (left and right), 27 (left and right), 28, 29
(right), 31, 33, 45, 47, 49, 53, 57, 65, 69, 72, 79,
80, 81, 83, 85, 90, 92

Contents

Foreword

John C. Whitehead

In 1987, when my art dealer friend Achim Moeller first suggested that we collaborate on a catalogue of my collection on the occasion of my sixty-fifth birthday, I balked.

In the first place, I thought that my "collection," as he called it, was not really that. It was rather an accumulation of things I'd acquired here and there over the previous twenty years. The word "collection" connotes some central purpose, some common theme, and my things unfortunately did not have that.

In the second place, my collection was not really all that good. It was presumptuous to think of it in the same order as the great private collections of French Impressionism and Post-Impressionism – Walter Annenberg, Chester Dale, the Havermeyers, the Garbishes. Even among current collectors of that period, my collection could not compare in scope and quality, and I thought it pretentious to aggrandize it with a catalogue.

Finally, my collection was far from finished. It was incomplete, and quite spotty. There were a few very good things, quite a few not so good things, and a few that really don't belong at all. I was still adding and subtracting, as my tastes and knowledge changed and developed, and as time and pocketbook permitted.

But in spite of all these reasons, I decided to go ahead. I thought some of my friends might enjoy seeing what I'd been up to in my spare time. Others, sensing what great joy I'd gained from art, might be encouraged to give it a go themselves.

Now, fifteen years later, I am quite willing to call it a "collection." It is better than it was then. Most of the misfits are gone; some of the gaps have been filled. While surely not up to the standards of "the great ones" and still not complete, it is the best I've been able to do in the time and with the resources available. And so I agreed with Achim that it might be time to show off some of it again.

It all started on an early summer night in London in 1978. Sotheby's was selling the great collection of Robert von Hirsch, the noted German collector who lived in

Switzerland. Tickets to the sale were hard to come by, but a friend found me two in the front row, and from then on I was hooked. Caught up in the spirit of the auction, I suddenly heard myself bidding. Silence immediately descended on the room. My bid had won, and I owned my first work of art. It was a Modigliani drawing, the head of a woman. Flushed with the success of my newfound acquisition, I returned to New York, the drawing under my arm, to find out who this Modigliani fellow was, what else he'd painted, and who his friends were. And so it began.

As the years passed, and as I found time to read about the period and the artists, to visit museums and galleries, I kept buying. I have never bought anything that I didn't love, that I didn't feel I'd enjoy looking at for the rest of my life. There is a temptation to buy things because someone thinks you "ought" to have them or because they seem to be bargains, but I've tried to resist that. Nevertheless, I'm constantly amazed at how my tastes change and develop, hopefully for the better. Things that I thought I loved some years ago, I don't love quite so much now, and there are still a few things that I can't believe I ever could have loved.

I have never bought anything solely because I thought it was a good investment, there are better opportunities elsewhere than in art. Having said that, fine works of art can be good investments. Almost everything that I have acquired could be sold today for a good deal more than I paid for it. That simple fact gives me courage to keep plunging ahead, even though prices of the best works often seem to be outrageously high.

I've never hesitated to seek all the guidance I can get when I'm thinking about a painting, although in the end I always make my own decisions. Achim Moeller, the dealer whose advice I've sought more than anyone else's in recent years, has saved me more than once from making a bad mistake, and he's brought a number of opportunities to my attention that I would not have known of otherwise. Best of all, he's been absolutely honest with his opinions and has never pushed me to do something I didn't want to do. I'm grateful to him for his help. While expressing thanks, I must also thank J. Carter Brown, Director Emeritus of the National Gallery of Art, and Charles F. Stuckey, an authority on French Impressionism, for their willingness to comment on the collection and for their generous remarks.

I had the misfortune to fall in love with a period of art where prices are particularly high. If I were starting over, I'd try to choose a less expensive mistress. Opportunities abound. I marvel that works of the great masters of many periods still seem to sell for very modest prices. As for the Impressionists, the greatest paintings of artists such as van Gogh, Cézanne, and Renoir are mostly in museums. When a work does come on the market, it brings many millions of dollars and is beyond my reach.

Nevertheless, it is still possible to find absolutely first-rate works by lesser artists, and, with patience and care, even by the greatest masters. So I continue to look. Part of the joy is the chase.

Now, fifteen years later, Achim and I are publishing again, this time a selection of some of the finest works that I have acquired, to celebrate my eightieth birthday. I thought it had only been a few years since we first started, but I was wrong. Where have the years gone!

The collection has changed, not so much in the objective as in the execution. It is larger, larger than I originally thought it would become, and larger than my walls can hold. I like to think its quality has also improved, but I realize there are still some gaps: no really major Cézanne, Toulouse-Lautrec, or van Gogh. We have weeded out half a dozen things that seemed to be repetitious or that just didn't wear well.

The collection has not only become fatter, but also broader in scope. It is still all French, but extends now from pre-Impressionism, like Corot, Courbet, and Daumier, to an occasional modernist, like Lehmbruck and Arp.

During my tour of duty in the State Department from 1985 to 1989, I moved some of my paintings to Washington, where they hung in my rather grand office, as well as in my apartment. Clem Conger, then the State Department's Curator of Art, was shocked that the Deputy Secretary of State would choose to have French art in his office, not American art. But I stood my ground and at least the French Ambassador, Bobby de Margerie, a former director of the Louvre, was very pleased.

I continue to be amused that many friends from my banking years at Goldman, Sachs and from my diplomatic years in the State Department are surprised when they learn that I collect art with some seriousness, in the same way that their eyes widen and their jaws drop when they hear that I used to play the violin or went on Outward Bound trips or that I owned part of the Devils hockey team. Collecting art seems to them a rather odd thing for me to do, incongruous and somehow out of character.

But I do still enjoy it. It's a refreshing break from everything else I do. I find that I like being surrounded by beautiful things, and it doesn't hurt that they also seem to increase in value as the years go by.

The search goes on. The collection is still very much in progress. I suppose that as long as I live, it will never be finished.

March 2002

John C. Whitehead

J. Carter Brown
Director Emeritus, National Gallery of Art

OK, I admit it. John Whitehead is my hero.

Every age needs heroes. Few, however, are as self-effacing and simultaneously effective as John C. Whitehead, now approaching his ninth decade.

In an age of celebrity, where we relish people who are famous just for being famous, John somehow has been able to keep an amazingly low profile, given all the visible concerns with which he has been connected. Personable of mien, he is quiet, and affable, and creates an impression of gentleness.

However, one does not chair as many organizations as he has without having a real grip on the realities, and an ability to shape a board, determine its priorities, and lead by example, personally doing some ineluctably effective fundraising.

His competence was shown as he rose to the top of Goldman Sachs, and then again when he was chosen by George Shultz in to be his Deputy Secretary of State, serving from 1985 to 1989. This appointment made John the Number Two in that vast, worldwide department, and he acted as Secretary of State with full powers when Shultz was traveling, which, given the Secretary's responsibilities, was a good deal of the time. Since the Secretary of State is ex-officio one of the nine trustees of the National Gallery of Art, it was nice to think of our having a friend at court. And he confesses that his government experience gave him a taste for public service, which has been his watchword ever since.

At the risk of being very personal, John Whitehead reminds me so of my own father, who felt that his service in Washington was the peak experience of his life, but who also, like John, devoted his energies to serving non-profit organizations and to philanthropy in a similarly gentle way. And my father not having been with us since 1979, I carry around the very idea of John as a kind of surrogate.

I got to know John during his membership in the National Gallery of Art's

Trustees' Council. It was wonderful to see him take on the chairmanship of the Andrew W. Mellon Foundation. That foundation has long commanded my total respect for its understanding of the role of private philanthropy – to fill in where the lemmings aren't running – and for maintaining the highest standards of intellectual probity and quality. Their support of the arts, and of universities and research libraries, helping to bring advanced scholarly research into the electronic age, has been exemplary. As John has been quoted as saying about serving on non-profit boards, "The first rule is to take it seriously. Don't go into it unless you are ready to devote the time, energy, and thought to make the organization succeed."

It is staggering to consider the list of organizations that he has served, more often than not as chair. Although lists can be boring, this one is so amazing that I do not hesitate to record it here. His chairmanships and former chairmanships include, as I have mentioned, The Andrew W. Mellon Foundation, but in addition, the Harvard Board of Overseers, Asia Society, Haverford College, International House, the International Rescue Committee, the Greater New York Councils of the Boy Scouts of America, the Goldman Sachs Foundation, and, no less, the Board of the Federal Reserve Bank of New York. He is vice-chairman of the United Nations Association of the U.S.A. Additional board memberships include or have included the J. Paul Getty Trust, the National Humanities Center, the Nature Conservancy, Lincoln Center Theater, the East-West Institute, Eisenhower Exchange Fellowships, and Rockefeller University. He is also a member of the Council on Foreign Relations. His Washington connections, in addition to the National Gallery of Art, are as Chairman Emeritus of the Brookings Institution and of Youth for Understanding. It boggles the mind.

I had the luck of being involved in one cause of his that was of particular interest to me. We are both graduates of the Harvard Graduate School of Business Administration. I was asked to attend a meeting in which he was outlining his vision that the Business School should serve to train leaders in the non-profit world as well as business. As I had been anomalously admitted, in the class of 1958, as the lone applicant to the school professing from the outset that his goal was cultural management, I was naturally delighted to hear of John's initiative. He backed it up with a fabulous $10 million grant to encourage the school in this direction.

John's insight was one that I have come to observe first hand. As John pointed out at that meeting, based on his experience in both realms, managing a not-for-profit organization is trickier than a for-profit one. In the latter, there is basically one bottom line, and the measurement of one's success is relatively simple. In the non-profit world, there are so many constituencies, and so many subjective criteria, that management

Gustave Caillebotte (1848–1894)
Bords de l'Yerres
(Banks of the Yerres)
circa 1878
Oil on board
5 ⅞ x 5 ⅝ inches (15 x 22 cm.)

can be especially challenging. Members of the staff who have the knowledge necessary for the substantive mission of the organization may not have had an opportunity to acquire the requisite management skills to run the place in a businesslike way. At the same time, these enterprises are not businesses.

Management is a means, not an end. So many trustees make the mistake, coming from their successes in the business world, of not realizing that the culture of a non-profit is sui generis, and needs to be handled with great sensitivity.

Sensitivity John Whitehead has. One mourns his late wife, recognizing what an extraordinary blow it must have been to him to have the beautiful Nancy Dickerson, brilliant White House correspondent and television personality, so thrilled with their new life, be stricken down so soon after their marriage. That he should have accomplished so much going forward after this blow is another tribute to his very special inner resources.

In a course in business history at the Harvard Business School, we studied the Medici as major innovative forces in the world of international banking, introducing double-entry bookkeeping, investing wisely, and amassing an important fortune. When, in our case history, it was revealed that Lorenzo de' Medici was also a poet and a major art collector, some classmates of mine simply could not process that idea. They found it almost impossible to conceive of anyone being a tough businessman and involved simultaneously in those namby-pamby arts. What they were learning about was of course what we have come to know as a "Renaissance man."

John Whitehead is just that. His interests are far ranging, including the New Jersey Devils hockey team and the challenging hardships of the Outward Bound program. No stranger to harm's way, he served in the Navy in World War II, participating in the invasions of Normandy and Southern France and Iwo Jima and Okinawa. But what

Camille Pissarro (1830–1903)
Pommiers en fleurs, Éragny
(Apple Blossoms, Éragny), circa 1900
Oil on panel 8 5/16 x 10 5/8 inches (21.1 x 26.8 cm.)

Aristide Maillol (1861–1944)
Study for 'La Montagne', 1936
Bronze, edition 2 of 6
10 7/8 x 11 3/8 x 4 3/4 inches (27.6 x 29 x 12 cm.)

Pablo Picasso (1881–1973)
Trois danseurs (Three Dancers), circa 1925
Pen and India ink on tan paper
14 3/8 x 10 1/2 inches (36.5 x 26.7 cm.)

endears him particularly to me is his sensitivity to art. His collection is not large, and not of the mold of so many tycoon collections where the owner is buying for the name and for the splash on the wall. His paintings, drawings, watercolors, and sculpture are, in the main, of an intimate scale, endowing them with a personal quality that makes one realize that they were bought for love. His eye, guided expertly by the knowledgeable Achim Moeller, has turned up some wonderful objects.

A brilliant analysis of the collection has been done by our former curator of modern paintings at the Gallery, Charles Stuckey. Suffice it to say here that I have many personal favorites. I have often thought that the best way to visit a museum is to apply what I call the "Cupidity Test," and to choose out those objects that one would most like to steal if one only could.

Obviously some of the larger paintings, like the Berthe Morisot, which was the linchpin of our monographic show of the artist at the National Gallery, or his fabulous Modigliani portrait, or the Maurice Denis, have that museum wall-power. So, too, the magnificent Redon flower piece, which he generously assigned to the Gallery in honor of its fiftieth anniversary. But it is the originality of finding arguably the best Stevens I know, even though small in scale, or recognizing Caillebotte's genius in a painting about the size of a postcard, that gives one the sense that there is a real eye at work here. Similarly, many works are totally endearing, such as the little Pissarro sketch of apple blossoms, or the small Bonnard. In the National Gallery's East Building, we insisted with the architect on some small, low-ceilinged galleries that could invoke the scale of a domestic setting. These rooms turned out to be perfect for the small French paintings, collected primarily by Ailsa Mellon Bruce, that are perennially among the most popular exhibits we offer. We have learned that to take them down for any reason incites so much protest that they have become a virtually permanent fixture among all the rotating

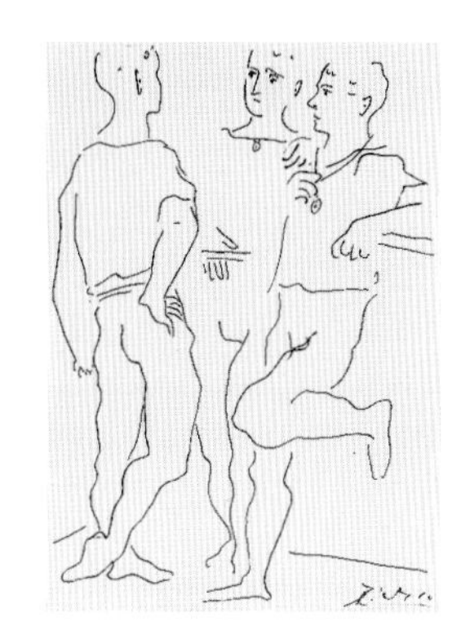

exhibits in the East Building. The Whitehead collection has so much the same appeal.

John's taste in sculpture exhibits the same sensitivity. The Rodin *Evil Spirits* is an important work, one of two, the other of which is at the National Gallery. But my favorites perhaps are the smaller works, the Bourdelle, the Lehmbruck, and the wonderfully monumental small version of the Maillol, *La Montagne.*

If a collector understands that small is beautiful, he is probably likely to be an important collector of works on paper, and this is certainly true in John's case. He has wonderful drawings by important artists like Degas, the early Van Gogh, and now two Seurats, one a study for a figure in Georges Seurat's masterpiece, the large Grande Jatte painting in Chicago, celebrated in Sondheim's "Sunday in the Park with George." His Gauguin fan also relates to a larger painting. But consider the quality of his little ink sketch by Forain, on no one's list of the most significant artists of the nineteenth century, and yet this spontaneous, economical sheet is as good as the artist gets. John's eye also takes him into the twentieth century, with a Braque and an impressive group of Matisse works on paper. His Picasso drawings impress us particularly with the economy of means of a simple pen. The wriggling rhythms inspired by Stravinsky are an absolute delight; and Picasso's *Three Dancers*, from that heroic classical period of the 1920s, shows that whatever other tricks that protean artist was up to over a long and varied career, he really could draw.

John has not stopped collecting, enriching his holdings since the 1997 show at Achim Moeller Fine Art with a wonderful array of acquisitions, many carrying out his theme of the small object of large quality. Take, for example, the small Matisse oil of 1918, the Laurens and Rodin bronzes, the small drawings by Pissarro and Toulouse-Lautrec, the supremely important Seurat conté crayon drawing, and the stenographic Manet ink wash sketch from the milieu of the artist's beloved theater.

Edouard Manet (1832–1883)
Quatre personnages au théâtre
(Four people at the Theater), circa 1880
Brush and India ink
4 ⅝ x 6 ¾ inches (11.8 x 17.2 cm)

Presently, John has agreed to accept Governor Pataki's appointment as Chairman of the new Lower Manhattan Development Corporation, which promises to be the largest rebuilding project that this city or any other has undertaken, with all the concomitant pressures from the varying interested parties. For someone with such a long and distinguished track record, needing not one ounce of additional glory, it is a decision close to sainthood that he should agree to take this project on.

We are all in John Whitehead's debt in so many ways. It is comforting that there are genuine heroes. I, unabashedly, consider him mine.

March 2002

Introduction to the John C. Whitehead Collection

Charles F. Stuckey

In the mid 1980s, when I was starting to organize a long overdue Berthe Morisot retrospective, I first saw *On the Veranda*, 1884, in an art gallery in New York. During her lifetime, the painter herself had chosen to exhibit this particular picture more frequently than any of her others. Therefore, I was determined to persuade whoever would acquire it to lend it as a centerpiece to this retrospective. That turned out to be John Whitehead, who did indeed agree to lend, and in the bargain invited me to enjoy his wonderful collection of early modern art. As the collection grows, so too does my admiration for it, both in its entirety and for the individual works it contains. It seems to me that the meanings of already familiar works, as well as new acquisitions, respond unavoidably to the context of the collection enjoyed as a whole. Already in 1987, Achim Moeller, Mr. Whitehead's devoted art consultant, invited me to provide a brief essay for a catalogue to celebrate "A Collection in Progress." A decade later I had the privilege to expand those first comments with respect to a greatly enhanced collection, and now it is my great pleasure to yet again revisit Mr. Whitehead's ever more delightful compendium of modern art.

Although the works in the Whitehead Collection have been selected for their unique qualities, nevertheless, it has always seemed to me that the coherence among the works says a great deal about the history of modern European art. To begin with, the mixture of works on paper and small sculptures with major paintings inevitably evokes the revolutionary contempt among modern-minded nineteenth-century artists for hierarchies based on genre or medium. During the mid-nineteenth century it became clear that rapid drawings, like those made by Daumier and Guys to illustrate newspapers, had the same potential for artistic greatness as the most elaborately refined works at monumental scale. Shortly after Morisot's death, for example, when her close friends organized a memorial showing of her work at a Paris gallery, Degas urged Monet and

Renoir to integrate her drawings and pastels with her oils, since she herself would have considered them all on par as art. Yet although Morisot and her Impressionist colleagues strove to make paintings with the spontaneity of colored drawings, and drawings with the virtuosity of oils, the idea of an integrated display of large and small, formal and informal works of art remains a rarity even today. Collections like Mr. Whitehead's thus provide a precious insight into the values at stake in the early years of modern art.

Mr. Whitehead's own personal favorite among all the works in his collection, Renoir's pastel of André Bérard, age eleven or so, epitomizes the modern dialogue between drawing and painting. Rendered throughout with scribbled lines, evidently so as not to overtax the patience of the young sitter, Renoir's portrait captures the bright airiness that the Impressionists were determined to record as a fact of visual experience ignored by art in the past. The sort of informal virtuosity on display in Renoir's portrait finds its match in Morisot's *On the Veranda*. Both charter members of the Impressionists' exhibition cooperative initiated in 1874, these artists became such close friends that after Morisot's death, Renoir practically adopted her orphaned daughter Julie into his own family.

Around age five, Julie served as her mother's model for *On the Veranda*, my favorite among the rich group of Impressionist works in the Whitehead Collection. This single work demonstrates Morisot's mastery of all three major pictorial categories: landscape, still-life, and figure. Captured in briskly animated brushwork, comparable to drawing with pastels, a faraway suburban landscape observed from an upper-story balcony serves as background for a genre scene of a child who is herself absorbed in the close-up observation of a floral still-life. Balzac claimed that a great writer ought to be able to convey the age, mood, and social status of any figure simply by observing it from the back. In apparent response, nineteenth-century artists, as Morisot does here, treated the figure from the back as a favorite theme, one potentially more revealing than

Odilon Redon (1840–1916)
Tête de jeune femme de profil
(Head of a Young Woman in Profile)
circa 1895
Pastel and pencil on brown paper
17 ¼ x 12 inches (43.9 x 30.5 cm.)

Henri Fantin-Latour (1836–1904)
Panier de fleurs
(Basket of Flowers)
1892
Oil on canvas
24 ¾ x 31 ½ inches (63 x 80.2 cm.)

any full frontal view. Morisot's primary subject here is the act of looking, and as viewers we look over her shoulder as she looks over the shoulder of her daughter. Watching the child's reverie on the play of sunlight encourages the picture's viewers to relish the artist's observations of animating light transforming the appearance of every line, surface, and texture. Morisot's stenographic observations record the richly poetic complexity of sensory experience.

On the table where Julie is seated are the elements of a traditional still-life painting composition. As it so happens, the Whitehead Collection includes a textbook example of the kind of painting that I have in mind, *Basket of Flowers*, a late still-life by Fantin-Latour. Similar glass pitchers with spiral fluting serve in each picture as touchstones by which to measure the quality and luster of light play. An associate of Morisot's in the avant-garde Paris art world from the mid-1860s on, Fantin gained international recognition for the richly orchestrated color harmonies in such floral still-life compositions, which are meticulously observed in sharp contrast against deep-toned backgrounds.

Observed in orthodox Impressionist fashion as manifold bits of shape and color, the still-life confronting Julie in the Morisot painting appears capriciously incomplete by Fantin-Latour standards. Yet both Fantin's photographic attention to physical details and Morisot's analytical attention to raw, disintegrated sensory data, prior to full conceptual recognition as particular physical entities, are equally marvelous to contemplate.

A promised gift to the National Gallery of Art, the mystical still-life by Redon in the Whitehead Collection might be described as something like an Impressionist Fantin-Latour. The vase of flowers in Redon's painting inhabits an indefinite otherworldly space, as if afloat in some primal dream ether. Descriptive of no physical facts, the delicate tones of yellow, pink, and violet in the airy background setting evoke perfumes

Roger de La Fresnaye (1885–1925)
Mon Ami, Jean Cocteau
1912
watercolor and pencil on light green paper
12 ¼ x 9 ¼ inches (31.1 x 23.5 cm.)

Pierre Bonnard (1867–1947)
Paysage stylisé (Le Grand-Lemps)
(Stylized Landscape, [Le Grand-Lemps])
circa 1890
Oil on canvas
13 ¾ x 9 ⅜ inches (34.9 x 23.8 cm.)

emanating from the flowers, under the artist's hallucinogenic observations.

Developed mostly in black and white images beginning around 1880, Redon's part-fact/part-fantasy subjects had enormous significance for Gauguin. By the late 1880s, Gauguin realized how to intensify such visionary drawings with color, in turn prompting Redon to revisit his early repertoire of images, but now with strange botanical color harmonies, such as those in the Whitehead Collection still-life. In his Brittany paintings of the late 1880s, Gauguin began to treat the background not as an exterior setting for his figures, but instead as an area in which to depict projections of their internal thoughts. Gauguin's reconsideration of the role of background had powerful implications for twentieth-century art. Predicated exclusively on sensory data, Impressionism had been unconcerned with invisible realms like feelings, memories, or fantasies. These concerns are evident in the fan in the Whitehead Collection, painted by Gauguin in Tahiti in 1892. The odd disparities of hairstyle, costume, and color intensity between the standing woman on the right in the foreground, and the other seated women on the left suggest that the background scene may be understood as an inside-out mental image projected from the mind of the foreground woman. There is something similar at issue in the exquisite pastel by Redon, datable to circa 1895. Rather than describing some locale, the yellow aura around the presumably allegorical female head in profile expresses the private mood of the externally expressionless model. The same modern dynamic plays a role in several other Symbolist works in the Whitehead Collection, notably Maurice Denis's *The Cook*, 1893. Apparently painted during the course of the artist's honeymoon in Brittany, this "portrait" shows his wife, Marthe Meurier, against a background scene from the *Gospel According to St. John*, with Christ seated at table and served by Mary and Martha. Thus the young bride's private meditations on her Biblical namesake are projected as background. Invisible inner temptations take physical shape as projections that all but suffocate the young female nude in Rodin's *The Evil Spirits*, 1899.

To my way of looking, the powerful visual device exploited in all these Symbolist works is the starting-off point for several remarkable early-twentieth-century pictures in the Whitehead Collection. For example, in one of the paintings by van Dongen the model's head is dominated by a hat accented with an enormous, albeit unidentifiable flower, which might suggest that she is under the spell of one of Baudelaire's evil blossoms. The other painting by van Dongen in the collection shows a woman with a mask-like face, her eyes closed as if to indicate how she looks inwardly, while a fiery toned background, like a Redon aura, suggests a mindscape of molten passions. Treated as foreground rather than as background, the most explicitly externalized inner vision is the one in de La Fresnaye's 1912 "portrait" of Cocteau. The poet's head rises up above a vision of a seated nude woman and her companion. The Whitehead Collection boasts three works by this brilliant, too often overlooked, artist.

As if in competition with Symbolist interest in inner visions, many late-Impressionist and Post-Impressionist paintings transcribe reality with increased poetic intensity. Several works in the Whitehead Collection exemplify the trend I have in mind, none more so than Caillebotte's influential *Chrysanthemums*, probably painted in 1892 or 1893. In conceptual terms, this close-up view of one of the beds in the artist's opulent garden is conceived as a microcosm for life forces pulsing with colors. After Caillebotte's death in 1894, Monet received a nearly identical *Chrysanthemums* painting (today in the Musée Marmottan, Paris) as a souvenir of his old friend. As much a still-life as a landscape, *Chrysanthemums* is closely related to Monet's own close-up images of the water lilies, begun a few years later in his own luxurious garden. While Monet probably deserves credit for initiating the landscape–still-life hybrid in some of his 1870s Argenteuil garden paintings, it was Vincent van Gogh (whose brother Theo was Monet's dealer), who gave this modern type its most powerful expression during the late 1880s, for example in his now famous painting of a bed of irises observed from close-up (today in The J. Paul Getty Museum, Los Angeles). Since this particular van Gogh painting was first owned by the writer Octave Mirbeau, who often played host to Caillebotte and Monet, it is not hard to imagine that Caillebotte took inspiration from Mirbeau's van Gogh for his *Chrysanthemums* and then, in turn, provided inspiration for Monet's *Water Lilies*.

Equally under the spell of van Gogh and his favorite Japanese woodblock print-makers, like Hiroshige, the early Bonnard painting in the Whitehead Collection transcribes a latticework of branches and apple blossoms viewed from close-up at twilight. A perfectly reasonable transcription of reality, Bonnard's painting nevertheless suggests a spell of enchantment cast by a harvest moon. Painted more than twenty years later,

Camille Pissarro (1830–1903)
L'Église de Kew
(Church at Kew)
1892
Oil on canvas
21 ⅝ x 18 ⅛ inches (55 x 46 cm.)

Gustave Courbet (1819–1877)
Le Château de Chillon
1873–74
Oil on canvas
21 ¼ x 25 ½ inches (54 x 65 cm.)

by which time Bonnard had settled at Vernonnet, not far from Monet at Giverny, *Under the Tree* recalls Morisot's *On the Veranda*, incorporating a little still-life, a seated figure, and a garden landscape. Bonnard would seem to be positioned on a veranda to look down on the table in the garden shaded by the tree whose trunk is visible at the right edge of the painting. Brightly colored in the intense sunlight, the blurred plant forms in the upper unshaded section of the composition would be indecipherable were it not for their proximity to the recognizable figure in the foreground, herself absorbed with a newspaper and thus oblivious to this fantastical display of abstract color and shape.

Of course, painters working out-of-doors in orthodox Impressionist fashion needed to post themselves underneath a shade tree or an umbrella while they worked. In many plein-air paintings the overhanging branch of the nearby tree intrudes into the composition as the most near-to-hand element. A case in point is Monet's luminous *Morning Landscape*, 1888, a transcription, observed through a lattice of overhanging leaves, of a lush green Giverny meadow dappled with lavender shadows. Although Monet did not develop this particular motif as one of his famous extended series, begun a few years later, *Morning Landscape* nonetheless has enormous significance. It is among the earliest of Monet's works with the sort of nearly square format he eventually used for many of his *Water Lilies* paintings, and thus can be understood as one of his earliest "décorations." The term indicates paintings designed to enhance an interior setting with a meditative mood of relaxation.

Barely visible in Monet's *Morning Landscape* is a footpath that extends from the immediate foreground deep into the distance. Such a pathway is a vestige of perhaps the most popular motif in the early-nineteenth-century French landscapes of Corot and the so-called Barbizon artists, who served as role models for the Impressionists. The Whitehead Collection includes one such Corot, as well as much later works by Pissarro's

friend, Vignon, and his follower, Loiseau, all featuring the unpaved country road as a sort of symbol for the itinerant landscape artists dedicated to creating a collective portrait of rural France. Recently added to the collection, Pissarro's exquisite *The Road to Port-Marly*, 1872, was seemingly painted from the middle of a not much traveled road, with a horse pulling a peddler's wagon towards the artist. As an Impressionist, Pissarro was committed to transcribing every detail of this everyday scene as promptly as possible, before the approaching horse disappears along the road and before the clouds overhead blow by. His minute notations have the complexity of a mosaic or jigsaw puzzle of differently shaped strokes, each calculated to match one of the manifold tones and shadows with perfect economy. Later Pissarro landscapes in the Whitehead Collection, such as *Church at Kew*, 1892, are rooted in the classic Impressionist mode originating with works like *Road to Port-Marly*. The rich strokes are pulled and twisted to catch every glint of ambient light so that the animated paint surface effectively gives the illusion of the rustling daylight observed quickly at a glance.

Among the pioneering advocates of such expressive brushwork in modern French landscape painting was Courbet, who invented the idea of working in series so important to Impressionism. The Whitehead Collection includes one of about twenty views of the Château de Chillon painted by Courbet near the end of this career. Although some scholars have mistakenly disparaged these late paintings as items made primarily for sale as souvenirs to tourist-collectors, Courbet's self-imposed exile near this Swiss site had nothing to do with sightseeing. He had just been released from prison for his role in the Republican uprising of Parisians against the puppet regime set up after France lost its war with Prussia. The shadowy, fatalistic mood evident in these paintings, arguably self-portraits by proxy, would have appealed not to tourists but to pilgrims venerating the Château in recognition of Louis de Bonnivard. Imprisoned here in the early sixteenth century for his efforts to keep the city of Geneva independent, Bonnivard had been captured in the Jura, which was the home of Courbet's family.

The selection of master drawings in the Whitehead Collection has been considerably enriched with the addition of *Politics*, from the group of watercolors made by Daumier for the art market in the early 1860s. Daumier's ostensible subject, a group of the cronies gathered to drink, smoke, and read newspapers, is without much special interest apart from their ordinariness and their comic self-contentment, but it provided the artist with the occasion to orchestrate a truly magnificent interplay of light and shadow. Seemingly careless and off-handed, Daumier's drawing here displays uncanny virtuosity. Shapeless shadows, doodled and scumbled, indicate the rustling foliage and define the contours of the tree in the foreground. Indeed, shadows have a life of their own in this drawing. The figure seated next to the tree is half obscured by shadow, while with only the faintest shading, the empty chair in the sun-struck middle ground has scarcely more presence than a ghost.

Politics enhances a rich group of works by Daumier in the Whitehead Collection, including another exceptional watercolor, this depicting the single figure of a lawyer in a spare interior setting. The isolated figure is another hallmark themes in Impressionist and Symbolist genre painting. Departing from the conventions of genre painting these single-figure images are epigrammatic, fragments designed to imply much fuller scenes familiar from everyday life. Based upon seventeenth- and eighteenth-century court portraits with theatrical gestures and costumes, the single figures in nineteenth-century French genre art portray types rather than individuals. Grimly robed in black, for example, Daumier's lawyer is reminiscent of characters in what Balzac, the great contemporary novelist, called "The Human Comedy" of real life. Apparently unaware that he is being observed, he stands outside of the courtroom, in order to study some papers. The dramatic light, along with the legal costume, give the impression of theater, whether comedy or tragedy left intentionally unclear. Famous for his newspaper cartoons, Daumier was, of course, unsurpassed in the virtuoso concision of his visual language. It is hardly surprising, therefore, that his ambitious watercolors rival contemporary works by such controversial painters as Manet, who, by eliminating all but the essential details of setting and gesture, sought to intensify the power of a visual image to convey observations from life.

The isolated figure served Caillebotte as a similarly modern idiom in his drawing of a well-dressed businessman with a high hat. The man's unbuttoned coat and his gesture, one hand pocketed and the other holding a short cane, suggest some leisurely man-on-the-town narrative, although Caillebotte has dispensed with any setting.

Vincent van Gogh (1853–1890)
Orphan Man with Top Hat, Eating
1882
Pencil on gray paper
18 ¼ x 9 ¾ inches (46.5 x 24.5 cm.)

Georges Seurat (1859–1891)
La promeneuse au manchon
(Strolling Woman with a Muff)
circa 1884
Conté crayon on paper
11 ⅞ x 9 ⅛ inches (30 x 23 cm.)

In terms of size and style, this particular drawing has a very close relationship to a group of individual figure studies made by Caillebotte in 1876 for the large Parisian genre paintings that he contributed to the third Impressionist exhibition the following year. These works initiated a mode of monumental modern-life painting that would soon inspire Seurat. Like these studies, the 1878 Whitehead drawing has a light grid, to facilitate its enlargement on to a canvas. This particular drawing was not, however, developed as a detail to be incorporated into a complex multi-figure composition. Instead, this drawing served as the basis for a painting of a single figure, not a portrait, but an ultra-modern life-sized fragment of modern life silhouetted against a modulated gray background completely void of details.

Determined to create modern art about the poor and for their benefit, the young van Gogh made his earliest lithographs in late 1882. He wanted to be able to disperse inexpensive multiple copies of his drawings of lonely single figures, such as old men observed in the almshouses of The Hague. However, his financial situation limited his productions as a printmaker. Thus, the Whitehead drawing of a dignified, top-hatted welfare recipient taking a spoonful of soup was never realized as a lithograph. Observed exclusive of any setting, the simple gesture establishes this man's identity with the whole of humanity. Paradoxically, van Gogh's mastery of this type of dark, solitary figure image, important to many early modern artists, should probably be taken as the starting-off point for the intensely bright landscapes – without any figures – that would become his greatest legacy as a painter.

Rounding out this group of dark images of individuals made between the 1860s and the 1880s are two haunting drawings of figures in silhouette by Seurat. One depicts a stylishly dressed woman as a stereotype altogether lacking in individual traits. Were it not for the fact that Seurat ever so briefly indicated her face, this figure could

Camille Pissarro (1830–1903)
Fiacres sur le Boulevard Montmartre
(Carriages on Boulevard Montmartre)
1897
Ink and Sepia wash on paper
6 ¾ x 8 ⅝ inches (17.1 x 21.9 cm)

pass for her own shadow. There is no clue to where she has been, where she is, or where she is headed. The second Seurat drawing in the Whitehead Collection depicts a portly man wearing a top hat and a long overcoat, the collar turned. His hands pocketed and his face hidden, the funeral figure presiding in a blank setting appears no less alienated than the female figure. Starting in the early 1880s Seurat specialized in such moody drawings made with greasy conté crayons on heavy-weave paper. Varying with virtuosity the amount of pressure that he applied, Seurat achieved a subtle range of black tones, always leaving pinpoints of the cream-colored paper visible to evoke the play of dim gaslight. Limiting his means of expression in daring modern fashion, Seurat, no less than Daumier or van Gogh before him, stresses abstract mood with minimal attention to character or situation. Works of this type exemplify a characteristically late-nineteenth-century icon of modern times, namely the self left on its own with itself.

By contrast to these dark figures, three masterful drawings of isolated female models in the Whitehead Collection are about whiteness, with its implications of purity and sensuality. The earliest in date is the ballet dancer by Degas. Of course, this drawing epitomizes the period obsession with figures observed from behind, and thus lacking such easily comprehensible details as gesture or facial expression to hold the viewer's interest. Even so, considering all the hatching lines along the model's graceless profile and arm, possibly included to suggest movement, Degas was apparently determined to draw attention to the gesture that is so hard to see in his drawing. Indeed, the apparent awkwardness of this mostly hidden gesture would seem to imply that Degas's particular goal here was the random observation in Impressionist fashion of a model caught off guard and unaware that she is being observed. The smudges of color at her feet heighten the impression of informality, and suggest that Degas never intended this drawing for public release. Yet this work has the distinction of being signed by the perfectionist

Edgar Degas (1834–1917)
Danseuse debout, vue de dos
(Standing Dancer, View of Back)
circa 1872
Pencil and chalk on paper
16 ½ x 12 ¼ inches (41.9 x 31.3 cm.)

Aristide Maillol (1861–1944)
Le Printemps
(Spring)
1910–11
Bronze, lifetime cast
67 ½ x 19 x 12 ½ inches (71 x 48 x 31.5 cm.)

artist, who only added his name to works on the rare occasions when he sold or exhibited them. In contrast to the Degas drawing, there is nothing awkward about the expression or gesture of the nude model observed from the rear in the Renoir drawing in the Whitehead Collection. Instead, the artist posed the model to simulate the decorum associated with classical sculptures of goddesses. The delicate lines scarcely disturb the marmoreal whiteness of the paper. The exquisite Rodin drawing of an isolated female figure is neither an attempt at unvarnished realism à la Degas nor an attempt to rival the classical past à la Renoir. Wishing for his figure drawings to be altogether unconventional, Rodin instructed his models to move freely about the studio without any special purpose in mind. The drawing in the Whitehead Collection records such a posing session, when the model grasped her foot, creating an unprecedented and pointless pose, beautiful for its abstract body rhythms. The economy of line with which Rodin captured the odd pose is astounding. The richness of the drawing is about his shading with watercolor and the scribbled indications of drapery and hair, suggesting that he raced with his hand to keep up with the briefly glimpsed beauty of the model in motion for art's sake.

The avoidance of obvious gesture is also characteristic of many early modern figure sculptures. As secretive and mysterious as the figures in Seurat's drawings, Bourdelle's *Woman Draped in Her Large Shawl*, 1889, epitomizes the tendency of late-nineteenth-century sculptors to austerely simplify their means of expression. Works like Bourdelle's introduced the columnar, or caryatid type used so often by early-twentieth-century sculptors, for example Maillol, with his allegorical statue *Spring*, 1911. Maillol and his colleagues sought to concentrate the expressive force of their figures with the torso, often omitting not only gestures, but heads and limbs as well. For these artists, ideal sculpture composition was meant to be limited to the subject's core. They joked that any part of a sculpture that would break off, if the work were rolled down a hill, was

Wilhelm Lehmbruck (1881–1919)
Kleine Sinnende
(Pensive Woman, small version)
1911
Stucco cast, glazed
21 x 6 ¼ x 7 inches (53.5 x 15.9 x 17.8 cm.)

Henri Matisse (1869–1954)
Femme à la nature morte
(Woman with Still Life)
1944
Ink on paper
20 ¼ x 15 ½ inches (51.5 x 39.5 cm.)

Henri Matisse (1869–1954)
Bateaux à Collioure
(Boats at Collioure)
1905
Watercolor on paper
6 x 9 ⅝ inches (15 x 24.5 cm)

extraneous to its core plastic power. The beautiful female figure by Lehmbruck, likewise datable to 1911, shares this neo-classical concept. Folding her arms onto herself, she resists any gesture to either dress or undress herself. Her attitude suggests by default that the garment around her legs is beyond her control, like a skink shell or cocoon being shed in the process of birth and awakening.

Yet another group of works in this collection amounts to a survey of line drawing from Constantin Guys, who Bauldelaire nominated as the exemplary painter of modern life in the 1860s, to Picasso and Matisse. Quick to realize that the invention of photography had liberated artists from the painstaking description of inessential details, the newspaper illustrator Guys used line to capture the flicker and movement of reality on the fly, something that no camera could yet do. The consummate dexterity and slightness of Guys's transcriptions set a challenge for subsequent artists, from Toulouse-Lautrec to Modigliani. If evident from quick sketches in the Whitehead Collection, both of these artists could conjure a face with the bare minimum of graphic effort.

The greatest modern master of line, however, must be Picasso, who never took a day off, drawing constantly and thus perfecting a spontaneity of linear inflection. The magnificent two-sided drawing he made for the sheet music of Stravinksy's *Ragtime* best reveals how far Picasso could go beyond his most accomplished predecessors. These complex images, one with two figures, the other with three, are tour-de-force lessons in the capacity of a single line. Starting at the hat of the fiddler, this magical line not only describes all the characters' faces, fingers, and fashions. It also manages, as if played by the hand of some maestro, to evoke foot-tapping rhythms. These interconnect the gestures of this duet in a linear web that traps visual cognates for every musical sign, from notes to staffs and G-clefs. *Ragtime* is perhaps the paramount example of Picasso's astounding single-line drawings that almost immediately inspired such artists as Cocteau and Calder.

The obvious counterpart to *Ragtime* in the Whitehead Collection is the intricate 1949 drawing of a woman's head by Picasso's greatest rival, Matisse. This work amounts to several drawings of the same model superimposed in rapid succession one over the other, the climax image indicated by the darkest outlines of her basic features. The lighter, more preliminary lines superficially describe the rich textures of the model's hair and costume. On a deeper level, they evoke a pulsing life-force sensed beneath her mask of reverie. Since the aggregate of lines darkens the sheet like conventional shading would, her mood seems pensive, even sad. Most important, the sensuous web of tentative and definitive notations is legible as a cinematic narrative of Matisse's own artistic process.

The Whitehead Collection is especially rich in Matisse drawings. Ranging from the sparkling joy of life in the Fauve watercolor of rowboats, to the sexual suspense in the Nice period odalisque, whose face is cropped off at the top of the drawing, to the mixed festive and tearful account of a model upstaged by a still-life, each drawing possesses its own distinct graphic mode and mood. With the landscape view just visible at the upper left (either a view out of a window or a landscape image by Matisse hanging on a wall), *Femme à la nature morte*, 1944, consolidates the three major pictorial categories – still-life, landscape, and figure – that Morisot had brought together sixty years before in *On the Veranda*. Limiting his graphic vocabulary to the curving line, noting edges of form defined by light, Matisse revisits in this extraordinary drawing the goals of the Impressionist artist at the beginning of the modern era. The sense of light they sought to convey with abbreviated pictorial means is brightened in works like this one, which bring the modern tradition to fruition.

1987/ revised and expanded February 1997 and March 2002

John C. Whitehead: The Collector and His Dealer

Achim Moeller

I wish I could say that my collector friend had sought me out, compelled by all he had heard about my expertise, keen eye, and unerring judgment. In fact, in the early summer of 1981 a violent thunderstorm drove John C. Whitehead into my London gallery for shelter. We spoke about art, about collecting, and about John's own budding collection. Knowing nothing of his reputation or position, I did know John Whitehead was an unusually interesting gentleman from New Jersey. When he wired me a week later, telling me he wanted to buy a Braque painting we had discussed, I was delighted to hop on a plane to New York and deliver the work in person. There John and I continued our conversation on collecting which has happily lasted more than twenty years.

I regard my relationship with John Whitehead and his with me as an estimable achievement, comparable to other noteworthy collector-dealer associations of the past century. John is a man of great intelligence, integrity, and taste. I have helped him, I believe, to develop a truly personal concept of quality, and in our unending search for excellence, I have seen his vision grow even stronger and more coherent.

Shortly after meeting John, I began to act on his behalf, searching and suggesting, dissuading and recommending. John has an astute understanding of the dealer's functions. If it is the collector's joy to fall in love with a work of art, it is the dealer's duty to temper emotion with professionalism and knowledge. Where the collector chooses for beauty's sake, the informed dealer makes certain that aesthetic value and market value are in balance to a greater or lesser extent. Art is more than an emotional investment after all, and collections do require careful management (no less than mutual funds). My role is to be aware of the gaps in a particular collection and to know the collector's taste. For any given painting, drawing, or sculpture it is my responsibility to guarantee the authorship, check the physical condition, and research the provenance and exhibition history.

Robert Delaunay (1885–1941)
Arc en Ciel (Rainbow)
1914
Encaustic on canvas laid on board
15 x 18 ⅞ inches (38 x 58 cm.)

As a rule, I prepare a detailed price analysis and market comparison for each work, determining its comparative quality as well as its rarity. While respecting the ultimate importance of my client's taste, I provide an overall assessment of a work's value. I am immensely grateful to John for his trust and faith in me for more than twenty years.

This publication and the exhibition it accompanies commemorate the celebration of John's eightieth birthday, an event in which I am delighted to participate. With my best wishes goes my hope that his collection will be a work in progress for many years to come. This occasion, incidentally, is an anniversary for me as well. Thirty years ago I became an independent dealer when I opened my own gallery in London. I am happy to mark this milestone in the company of John Whitehead. He has my warmest thanks for parting with a selection of his works during this exhibition. I trust this very fine personal collection will inspire other collectors to embark on or persist in collecting, one of the most joyous of human activities.

March 2002

1

Honoré-Victorin Daumier (1808–1879)

Avocat (Avant l'audience)
(Lawyer [Before the Hearing])
circa 1863–65

Charcoal, pen and brush and India ink,
pastel and watercolor on paper laid down on card
15 x 11 ¼ inches (38 x 28.5 cm.)
Signed lower left: *h.D.*

2

Honoré-Victorin Daumier (1808–1879)

Buveurs de bière (La Politique)
(Beer Drinkers [Politics])
circa 1865

Pen and ink and watercolor on paper
14 ⅝ x 11 ⅛ inches (37.2 x 28.3 cm.)
Signed lower left: *h. Daumier*

h. Daumier

3

Camille Pissarro (1830–1903)

La Route de Port-Marly
(The Road to Port-Marly)
1872

Oil on paper laid on canvas
8 ½ x 11 ¼ inches (21.5 x 28.5 cm.)
Signed and dated lower left: *C. Pissarro 72*

C. Pissarro. 70

4

Gustave Caillebotte (1848–1894)

Étude pour le "Portrait de Paul Hugot"
(Study for "Portrait of Paul Hugot")
1878

Pencil on paper
18 ¼ x 11 ⅞ inches (46.3 x 28.5 cm.)
Atelier stamp lower left: *G. Caillebotte*

5

Georges Seurat (1859–1891)

Le Haut de Forme
(The Top Hat)
1883–84

Conté crayon on Michallet wove paper
12 ⅛ x 9 inches (31 x 23 cm.)

6

Berthe Morisot (1841–1895)

Dans la véranda or Sous la véranda
(On the Veranda)
1884

Oil on canvas
31 ⅞ x 39 ⅜ inches (81 x 100 cm.)
Signed lower left: *Berthe Morisot*

7

Claude-Oscar Monet (1840–1926)

Paysage de matin (Giverny)
(Morning Landscape [Giverny])
1888

Oil on canvas
28 ⅞ x 31 ¾ inches (73.4 x 80.7 cm.)
Signed and dated lower right: *Claude Monet 88*

8

Pierre-Auguste Renoir (1841–1919)

Portrait of a Young Boy (André Bérard)
1889–90

Pastel on paper
16 ¾ x 12 ¼ inches (42.6 x 31.1 cm.)
Signed upper right: *Renoir*

Renoir

9

Paul Gauguin (1848–1903)

Fan decorated with motifs from Ta-Matete (The Market)
1892

Graphite, gouache, watercolor, and ink on cream wove paper
5 ¾ x 18 ⅛ inches (14.5 x 46 cm.)
Dedicated, signed, and dated lower left:
à M^{de} Goupil hommage respectueux - P. Gauguin 1892

10

Gustave Caillebotte (1848–1894)
Massif de chrysanthèmes, jardin du Petit-Gennevilliers
(Clump of Chrysanthemums, Garden at Petit-Gennevilliers)
1893

Oil on canvas
39 ⅛ x 24 ⅛ inches (99.3 x 61.3 cm.)

Promised gift to the Metropolitan Museum of Art, New York.

11 **Maurice Denis (1870–1943)**

La cuisinière
(The Cook)
1893

Oil on canvas
31 ½ x 23 ⅝ inches (80 x 60 cm.)
Signed with the vertical monogram and dated lower left:
MAVD 93

12

Odilon Redon (1840–1916)

Bouquet de fleurs
(Bouquet of Flowers)
circa 1912

Oil on canvas
28 ¾ x 21 ½ inches (73 x 54.6 cm.)
Signed lower left: *Odilon Redon*

Promised gift to the National Gallery of Art, Washington, D.C.

13

Auguste Rodin (1840–1917)

Étude de femme nue
(Study of a Female Nude)
late 1890s

Pencil and reddish-brown watercolor on buff paper
12 ⅞ x 9 ¾ inches (32.7 x 24.8 cm.)
Signed lower right: *A Rodin*

14

Auguste Rodin (1840–1917)

Les Mauvais Génies
(The Evil Spirits)
1899

White marble, unique
24 x 14 ⅜ x 17 1/2 inches (61 x 36.5 x 44.5 cm.)
Signed on base: *A. Rodin*

15

Kees van Dongen (1877–1968)

La femme à l'aigrette
(Woman with a Plume)
circa 1910

Oil on canvas
21 ¾ x 18 ¼ inches (55.2 x 46.3 cm.)
Signed upper left: *van Dongen*

van Dongen

16

Amedeo Modigliani (1884–1920)

Portrait de Béatrice Hastings
1916

Oil on canvas
25 9/16 x 18 1/8 inches (65 x 46 cm.)
Signed and dated upper right: *Modigliani 1916*

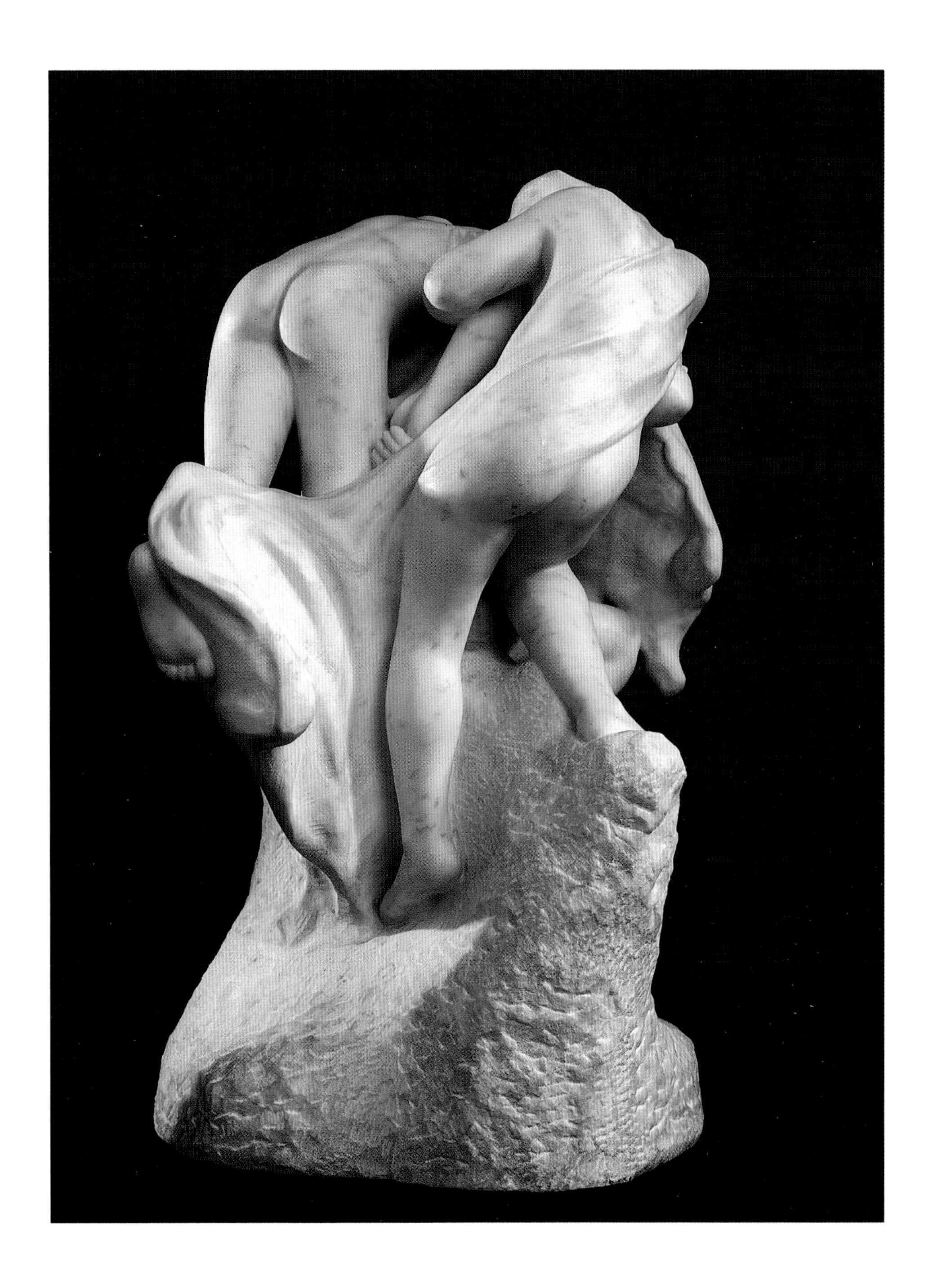

modigliani
1916

17

Pablo Ruiz Picasso (1881–1973)

Ragtime—Two Musicians, for Igor Stravinsky (recto)
Three Musicians (verso)
Projet pour la couverture de la partition de "Ragtime" d'Igor Stravinsky
(Design for the Cover of the Score of Igor Stravinsky's "Ragtime")
1918–19

Pen and ink on paper
10 ¾ x 7 ¼ inches (26 x 18.5 cm.)
Signed lower right: *Picasso*

18

Georges Braque (1882–1963)

Tête de femme II
(Head of a Woman II)
also Profils (Profiles)
1930

Oil on canvas
18 x 15 inches (45.7 x 38.1 cm.)
Signed and dated lower right: *G Braque 30*

G Braque
30

19

Henri Matisse (1869–1954)

Tête de jeune fille
(Head of a Girl)
1949

Charcoal on laid paper
16 x 12 inches (40.7 x 30.7 cm.)
Signed and dated lower right: *H. Matisse 49*

H Matisse 49

20

Henri Matisse (1869–1954)

Nature morte, pêches et verre (Still Life, Peaches and Glass) circa 1918

Oil on canvas
8 ⅞ x 10 ⅞ inches (22.5 x 27.7 cm)
Signed lower left: *Henri Matisse*

1 **Honoré-Victorin Daumier (1808–1879)**
Avocat (Avant l'audience)
(Lawyer [Before the Hearing])
circa 1863–65

Charcoal, pen and brush and India ink, pastel and watercolor on paper laid down on card
15 x 11 ¼ inches (38 x 28.5 cm.)
Signed lower left: *h.D.*

Provenance:

P. Aubry, Paris (George Petit: Vente P.A., Paris, May 10, 1897, Lot No. 42)
Durand-Ruel, Paris
Madame Esnault-Pelterie, Paris
Private Collection, Paris (Sotheby's, London, December 3, 1991, Lot No. 3)

Exhibitions:

Paris, Galerie Durand-Ruel, *Exposition des peintures et dessins de H. Daumier,* 1878, no. 100.
Paris, Musée de l'Orangerie, *Daumier: Peintures, aquarelles, dessins,* 1934, no. 128.
AMFA, NY, *The Whitehead Collection,* 1997.

Literature:

Arsène Alexandre, *Honoré Daumier: l'Homme et l'œuvre.* Paris, 1888, p. 378.
Catalogue de la Vente P. Aubry. Paris, May 10, 1897, Lot No. 42.
Das Museum. Leipzig, n.d. (circa 1910), no. 99, illustrated.
Erich Klossowski, *Honoré Daumier.* Munich, 1923, p. 97, no. 117, catalogued (titled *La Lecture au Placet*).
Michael Sadleir, Daumier: *The Man and the Artist.* London, 1924, pl. 34, illustrated.
Eduard Fuchs, *Der Maler Daumier.* Munich, 1930, p. 55, no. 204a, catalogued, pl. 204, illustrated.
B. Fleischmann and M. Sachs, *Honoré Daumier.* Vienna 1937 and Paris 1939, pl. 18, illustrated.
Raymond Escholier, *Daumier.* Paris, 1938, p. 73, illustrated.
Jean Cassou, *Daumier.* Lausanne, 1949, pl. 15, illustrated.
Marseille, Revue municipale. Vol. 3. Marseille, 1956, p. 41, no. 29, illustrated.
K. E. *Maison, Catalogue Raisonné of the Paintings, Watercolours and Drawings.* Vol. 2. London, 1968, p. 192, no. 577, catalogued, pl. 207, illustrated.
Claude Roy, *Daumier.* Geneva, 1991, p. 34, illustrated.
Colta Ives, Margaret Stuffmann, and Martin Sonnabend, *Daumier Drawings.* New York: Harry N. Abrams, Inc., 1992, p. 178, no. 114, illustrated (dated c. 1865); published in conjunction with the exhibition held at the Städelsche Kunstinstitut and Städtische Galerie, Frankfurt, November 17, 1992–January 17, 1993 and at The Metropolitan Museum of Art, New York, February 26–May 2, 1993.
AMFA, NY, 1997, pp. 19–20, no. 3, illustrated in color.

2

Honoré-Victorin Daumier (1808–1879)
Buveurs de bière (La Politique) (Beer Drinkers [Politics]) circa 1865

Pen and ink and watercolor on paper
14 5/8 x 11 1/8 inches (37.2 x 28.3 cm.)
Signed lower left: *h. Daumier*

Note: According to Dr. Michael Pantazzi, Associate Curator of European and American Art at the National Gallery of Canada, the Winterthur drawing is a preliminary version of the superior Whitehead drawing.

Provenance:

P. Aubry, Paris (George Petit: Vente P.A., Paris, May 10, 1897, Lot No. 41)
[Camentron]
[Durand-Ruel, Paris]
O. Gerstenberg, Berlin
[Matthiesen]
Albert Ch. Nussbaumer, Lugano (Sotheby's, London, June 28, 1999, Lot. No. 27.)

Exhibitions:

Beaux-Arts, 1901.
Galerie Rosenberg, no. 2, 1907.
London, National Gallery, *French Art of the 19th Century,* no. 26, 1943.
London, Tate Gallery, *Daumier: Paintings and Drawings,* exhibition organized by the Arts Council of Great Britain, June 14–July 30, 1961, no. 127, pl. 25a, illustrated.
Ingelheim am Rhein, *Daumier Drawings,* April 24–May 31, 1971.

Literature:

Catalogue de la Vente P. Aubry. Paris, May 10, 1897, Lot No. 41.
Kunst und Künstler. Berlin, 1911, p. 185.
Erich Klossowski, *Honoré Daumier.* Munich, 1923, p. 262, pl. 104, illustrated.
Raymond Escholier, *Daumier, peintre et lithographe.* Paris: Floury, 1923, p. 169, illustrated.
Michael Sadleir, *Daumier: The Man and the Artist.* London: Halton and Smith, 1924, pl. 52, illustrated.
Eduard Fuchs. *Der Maler Daumier.* Munich: Albert Langen, 1930, fig. 217a, illustrated.
Lassaigne, Jacques, *Daumier.* Paris: Hypérion, 1938, pl. 51, illustrated.
Jean Cassou, *Daumier* (mistakenly listed as being in the Reinhart Collection). Lausanne, 1949, pl. 20, illustrated.
Curt von Schweicher, *Daumier.* Paris: Aimery Somogy, 1953, pl. 11, illustrated.
K.E. Maison, *Burlington Magazine* (May 1956): p. 165, fig. 51, illustrated.
Gerhart Ziller, *Honoré Daumier.* Dresden: Verlag der Kunst, 1957, pl. 100, illustrated.
K.E. Maison, *Honoré Daumier: Catalogue Raisonné of the Paintings, Watercolours and Drawings.* Vol. 2. New York: NYGS, 1968, p. 9, pl. 93, illustrated.
Roger Passeron, *Daumier: Témoin de son Temps.* Paris: Bibliothèque des Arts, 1986, p. 279, illustrated in color.

3 **Camille Pissarro (1830–1903)**
La Route de Port-Marly
(The Road to Port-Marly)
1872

Oil on paper laid on canvas
8 ½ x 11 ¼ inches (21.5 x 28.5 cm.)
Signed and dated lower left: *C. Pissarro 72*

Provenance:

Gaston Bernheim de Villers, Paris
Private collection, Paris
(Sotheby's, London, June 29, 1999, Lot No. 110.)

Literature:

Ludovic-Rodo Pissarro & Lionello Venturi, *Camille Pissarro, son art-son œuvre.* Vol. 2. Paris, 1939, pl. 34, no. 168, illustrated.

4 **Gustave Caillebotte (1848–1894)**
Étude pour le "Portrait de Paul Hugot"
(Study for "Portrait of Paul Hugot")
1878

Pencil on paper
18 ¼ x 11 ⅞ inches (46.3 x 28.5 cm.)
Atelier stamp lower left: *G. Caillebotte*

Provenance:

Family of the artist
Private Collection, Paris
[Brame et Lorenceau]

Exhibitions:

Houston, The Museum of Fine Arts, *Gustave Caillebotte: A Retrospective Exhibition,* October 22, 1976–January 2, 1977; New York, Brooklyn Museum of Art, February 12–April 24, 1977. Catalogue by J. Kirk T. Varnedoe and Thomas P. Lee, no. D25, illustrated.
Paris, Galerie Brame et Lorenceau, *Gustave Caillebotte: Dessins, études, peintures,* February 28–March 24, 1989, pl. C, illustrated.
New York, Achim Moeller Fine Art, *Private Views: 19th and 20th Century European and American Masters. Fifth Anniversary Exhibition*, March 20–May 13, 1989, no. 1, illustrated on back cover.

Literature:

cf. Marie Berhaut, *Caillebotte, sa vie et son œuvre, Catalogue raisonné des peintures et pastels.* Paris: Fondation Wildenstein, Bibliothèque des Arts, 1978.
No. 81, *Portrait de Paul Hugot,* 1878, Oil on canvas, Collection Mr. and Mrs. Joseph E. Levine, New York (Private Collection, Lausanne), pp. 52, 109, illustrated in color.
No. 81A, *Paul Hugot,* drypoint etching, Collection Musée des Beaux-Arts de la Ville de Paris, p. 109, illustrated.
Kirk Varnedoe, *Gustave Caillebotte.* New Haven and London: Yale University Press, 1987, p. 118, no. 30A, illustrated. (French edition published by Adam Biro, Paris, 1988).
Jean Chardeau, *Les dessins de Caillebotte.* Paris: Editions Hermé, 1989, p. 82, illustrated.
To be included in the revised edition of the catalogue raisonné in preparation by Sophie Pietri, Wildenstein Institute, Paris.

5 **Georges Seurat (1859–1891)**
Le Haut de Forme
(The Top Hat)
1883–84

Conté crayon on Michallet wove paper
12 ⅛ x 9 inches (31 x 23 cm.)

Provenance:

Léon Appert (1837–1925), Paris, as of 1908; by inheritance to his daughter, Madame Léon Roussel, Paris
Ian Woodner, New York, as of 1988
The Woodner Family Collection, New York
[Wildenstein Gallery]

Exhibitions:

Paris, Galerie Bernheim-Jeune, *Retrospective Georges Seurat,* December 14, 1908–January 9, 1909, no. 159 (reprinted in C.M. de Hauke, 1961).
Paris, Musée Jacquemart-André, Seurat, November–December 1957, no. 46.
New York, The Metropolitan Museum of Art, *Master Drawings from the Woodner Collection,* March 10–May 13, 1990, no. 132, illustrated in color.
Paris, Grand Palais, *Seurat* (cat. by R.L. Herbert, F. Cachin, et al.), April 9–August 12, 1991, no. 47, illustrated in color; New York, The Metropolitan Museum of Art, September 24, 1991–January 12, 1992, no. 48 (American edition of catalog).

Literature:

Bulletin de la Vie Artistique, 1 September 1921, p. 472, illustrated.
Lucie Cousturier, *Georges Seurat.* Paris: Cres, 1926, pl. 46, illustrated.
D.C. Rich, *Seurat and the Evolution of La Grande Jatte.* Chicago, 1935, pp. 15, 18, 10, notes 1, 10, 13.
André Lhote, *Seurat.* Paris, 1948, pl. 4, illustrated.
C.M. de Hauke, *Seurat et son œuvre.* Paris, 1961, vol. 1, p. 242 (facsimile of Bernheim-Jeune catalog); vol. 2, pp. 150–151, no. 57, fig. 571, illustrated.
R.L. Herbert, *Seurat's Drawings.* New York, 1962, pp. 117–19, 182, no. 101, illustrated in color.
Paris, Hôtel George V, *Importants tableaux des XIX et XX siècles...*, June 22, 1988, Lot 4, illustrated in color.
John Russell, "Seurat Beckons to Many Worlds Beyond the Dot." *The New York Times* (Art View), 28 April 1991, illustrated.
R. Kendall, "Highlights and Shadows: Seurat Retrospective at the Grand Palais." *Apollo* 133, no. 352 (June 1991): p. 420, illustrated.
M.F. Zimmermann, *Seurat.* Weinheim, Germany, 1991, pp. 127–129, no. 252, fig. 252.

6 **Berthe Morisot (1841–1895)**
Dans la véranda or **Sous la véranda**
(On the Veranda)
1884

Oil on canvas
31 ⅞ x 39 ⅜ inches (81 x 100 cm.)
Signed lower left: *Berthe Morisot*

Provenance:

Ernest Chausson, Paris, 1929 (His sale, June 5, 1938, Lot. No. 33, illustrated.)
Private Collection, Paris
Galerie Schmit, Paris
[Acquavella Galleries]

Exhibitions:

Paris, *Exposition Internationale de peinture,* May 1887, no. 99.
Paris, Boussod-Valadon, *Berthe Morisot,* May–June 1892, no. 7.
Brussels, *La Libre Esthétique,* March 1894, no. 320.
Paris, Galerie Durand-Ruel, *Berthe Morisot,* March 5–21, 1896, no. 28.
Paris, Grand Palais, *Salon d'Automne,* October 1–22, 1907, no. 144.
Pittsburgh, Carnegie Institute, *Exhibition of Paintings: Edouard Manet, Pierre Renoir, Berthe Morisot,* October 15–December 1, 1924, no. 14.
Chicago, Art Institute of Chicago, *Paintings by Berthe Morisot,* January 30–March 10, 1925, no. 7.
Paris, Galerie Bernheim-Jeune, *Berthe Morisot au Cercle de la Renaissance,* 1929, no. 51.
London, M. Knœdler & Co., *Berthe Morisot,* May–June, 1936, no. 1.
Washington, D.C., National Gallery of Art, *Berthe Morisot: Impressionist,* organized by Charles F. Stuckey, September 6–November 29, 1987; Fort Worth, Kimbell Art Museum, December 14, 1987–February 22, 1988; South Hadley (Mass.), Mount Holyoke College Art Museum, March 14–May 9, 1988. Catalogue by Charles F. Stuckey and William P. Scott, assisted by Suzanne Glover Lindsay, New York: Hudson Hills Press, 1987, p. 104, no. 51, illustrated in color.
Montclair, 1989, p. 13, no. 49, illustrated.
AMFA, NY, *The Whitehead Collection,* 1997.
Washington, D.C., The Phillips Collection, *Impressionist Still Life,* September 22, 2001–January 13, 2002; Boston, Museum of Fine Arts, February 17–June 9, 2002; catalogue by Eliza Rathbone and George Shackelford, New York: Harry N. Abrams, 2001, pp. 150–51, illustrated in color.

Literature:

"Petites Expositions: L'œuvre de Berthe Morisot." *La Chronique des arts et de la curiosité, supplément à la Gazette des Beaux-Arts,* no. 11, 14 March 1896, p. 98.

Camille Mauclair, *Maîtres d'hier et d'aujourd'hui.* Paris, 1907, p. 318.

Louis Rouart, "Berthe Morisot." *Art et Décoration* 9 (May 1908): p. 176.

Monique Angoulvent, *Berthe Morisot.* Paris: Editions Albert Morancé, n.d. (1933), p. 100, no. 151.

Denis Rouart, *Correspondance de Berthe Morisot.* Paris: Quatre-Chemins-éditart, 1950, p. 168.

Denis Rouart, *Berthe Morisot.* Paris: Les Editions Braun et Cie, 1954, no. 34, illustrated.

M.-L. Bataille and G. Wildenstein, Berthe Morisot, *Catalogue des peintures, pastels et aquarelles.* Paris: Les Beaux-Arts editions d'études et des documents, 1961, p. 33, no. 160, pl. 57, illustrated.

Julie Manet, *Journal (1893–1899).* Paris: Klinsieck, 1979, p. 88.

Jean Dominique Rey, *Berthe Morisot.* New York: Crown Publishers, Inc., 1982, pp. 42, 62, illustrated in color.

Kathleen Adler, "Berthe Morisot at the National Gallery, Washington, D.C." *Burlington Magazine* 129, no. 87 (November 1987): pp. 765–67, illustrated.

AMFA, NY, 1987, pp. 68–69, illustrated in color.

Anne Higonnet, *Berthe Morisot, une biographie.* Paris: Adam Biro, 1989, pp. 200, 220.

Suzanne Glover Lindsay, "Berthe Morisot: Nineteenth-Century Woman as Professional," in *Perspectives on Morisot,* ed. T.J. Edelstein. New York: Hudson Hills Press in association with The Mount Holyoke College Art Museum, 1989, pp. 84–85, no. 16, illustrated in color.

J.-J. Levêque, *Les années impressionnistes.* Paris, 1990, p. 474, illustrated.

AMFA, NY, 1997, pp. 44–47, no. 35, illustrated in color.

Alain Clairet, Delphine Montalant, and Yves Rouart, *Berthe Morisot, 1841–1895: Catalogue raisonné de l'œuvre peint.* Paris: CERA-NRS, 1997.

Eliza Rathbone and George Shackelford, *Impressionist Still Life.* New York: Harry N. Abrams in association with the Phillips Collection, 2001, pp. 150–51, illustrated in color.

To be included in the forthcoming revised catalogue raisonné in preparation by Sophie Pietri, Wildenstein Institute, Paris.

7 **Claude-Oscar Monet (1840–1926)**
Paysage de matin (Giverny)
(Morning Landscape [Giverny])
1888

Oil on canvas
28 ⅞ x 31 ¾ inches (73.4 x 80.7 cm.)
Signed and dated lower right: *Claude Monet 88*

Provenance:

Mrs. James F. Sutton, New York
(Her sale, American Art Association, New York, October 26, 1933, Lot No. 56, illustrated)
Chester Dale, New York
George Roberts
Mrs. Donald Roberts Arthur (Sotheby's, New York, May 14, 1985, Lot No. 29)

Exhibitions:

New York, The Metropolitan Museum of Art, *Monet's Years at Giverny: Beyond Impressionism,* (also traveled to St. Louis Art Museum). Exhibition catalogue, New York: Harry N. Abrams, Inc., 1978, no. 8, illustrated in color.
Montclair, 1989, p. 9, no. 48, illustrated.
AMFA, NY, *The Whitehead Collection*, 1997, illustrated on cover.

Literature:

Gustave Geoffroy, *La vie artistique, Histoire de l'Impressionnisme*. Vol. 2. Paris, 1894, p. 86.
Gustave Geoffroy, *Claude Monet: sa vie, son temps, son œuvre*. Paris, 1922, p. 283.
Daniel Wildenstein, *Claude Monet: Biographie et catalogue raisonné, Vol. III: 1887–1898, Peintures*. Lausanne–Paris: Bibliothèque des Arts, 1979, pp. 114–15, no. 1205, illustrated.
AMFA, NY, 1987, p. 66–67, illustrated in color.
Daniel Wildenstein, *Monet: Catalogue raisonné, Vol. V: Supplement aux peintres, dessins, pastels, index*. Lausanne: Wildenstein Institute, 1991, p. 46.
Daniel Wildenstein, *Monet: Catalogue Raisonné-Werkverzeichnis*. Vol. 3. Köln: Taschen-Wildenstein Institute, 1996, pp. 457–58, no. 1205, illustrated.
AMFA, NY, 1997, p. 58–59, no. 41, illustrated in color.

8 **Pierre-Auguste Renoir**
(1841–1919)
Portrait of a Young Boy
(André Bérard)
1889–90

Pastel on paper
16 ¾ x 12 ¼ inches (42.6 x 31.1 cm.)
Signed upper right: *Renoir*

Provenance:

Pierre Renoir
Galerie Barbazanges, Paris, 1927
Galerie Alfred Flechtheim, Berlin, 1928
Private Collection, Germany
Neuberger Collection, Germany
[Sayn-Wittgenstein]

Exhibitions:

Berlin, Galerie Alfred Flechtheim, *Renoir,* October 7–November 9, 1928, p. 12, no. 37, illustrated.
Montclair, 1989, no. 60.
AMFA, NY, *The Whitehead Collection*, 1997.

Literature:

AMFA, NY, 1987, pp. 84–85, illustrated in color.
AMFA, NY, 1997, pp. 66–67, no. 45, illustrated in color.
François Daulte, *Auguste Renoir, Catalogue Raisonné de l'Œuvre: Pastels, Aquarelles et Dessins.* Vol. 6. Illustrated.

9 **Paul Gauguin (1848–1903)**
Fan decorated with motifs from Ta-Matete (The Market)
1892

Graphite, gouache, watercolor, and ink on cream wove paper
5 ¾ x 18 ⅛ inches (14.5 x 46 cm.)
Dedicated, signed, and dated lower left: *à Mde Goupil hommage respectueux - P. Gauguin 1892*

Provenance:

Collection Vaïté Goupil, Papeete, Tahiti
G. Courvoisier, The Penthouse Gallery, San Francisco, 1938
Mrs. Richard Rheem, San Fransisco
David Page, Paris
[Beadleston Gallery]

Exhibitions:

Washington, D.C., National Gallery of Art, *The Art of Paul Gauguin*, organized by Richard Brettell, Françoise Cachin, and Charles F. Stuckey, April 17–July 31, 1988; Chicago, The Art Institute of Chicago, September 7–December 10, 1988; Paris, Musée d'Orsay, January 10–April 20, 1989, no. 133.
Montclair, no. 39.
AMFA, NY, *The Whitehead Collection*, 1997.
New York, The Metropolitan Museum of Art, *Gauguin / New York,* June 18–October 20, 2002.

Literature:

cf. Ronald Pickvance, *The Drawings of Gauguin.* London: Paul Hamlyn, 1970, pp. 8, 19 (discussion of fans).
cf. Marc S. Gernstein, "Paul Gauguin's 'Arearea.'" The Museum of Fine Arts, Houston, *Bulletin* 7, no. 4 (Fall 1981): pp. 2–18 (discussion of fans).
AMFA, NY, 1987, pp. 54–55, illustrated in color.
AMFA, NY, 1997, pp. 76–78, no. 52, illustrated in color.
Achim Moeller, *In Good Hands: 25 Years of Art in the Life of a Dealer.* New York: Achim Moeller Fine Art, 1997, pp. 24–25, 71–72.
To be included in volume two of the forthcoming catalogue of pastels, gouaches, and drawings of Paul Gauguin now in preparation by the Wildenstein Institute, Paris.

10 **Gustave Caillebotte (1848–1894)**
Massif de chrysanthèmes, jardin du Petit-Gennevilliers (Clump of Chrysanthemums, Garden at Petit-Gennevilliers) 1893

Oil on canvas
39 ⅛ x 24 ⅛ inches (99.3 x 61.3 cm.)

Promised gift to the Metropolitan Museum of Art, New York.

Provenance:

Ira Spanierman, New York, 1970
C.K. Lock, New York, 1971
Private Collection
[Marlborough Gallery]
[Barbara Guggenheim]

Exhibitions:

Houston, The Museum of Fine Arts, *Gustave Caillebotte: A Retrospective Exhibition,* October 22, 1976–January 2, 1977; New York, Brooklyn Museum of Art, February 12–April 24, 1977. Catalogue by J. Kirk T. Varnedoe and Thomas P. Lee, 1976, pp. 32, 178, no. 74, illustrated in color.
New York, Marlborough Gallery Inc., *Masters of the 19th and 20th Centuries,* May 7–June 11, 1983, no. 6, illustrated.
Montclair, 1989, no. 11.
AMFA, NY, *The Whitehead Collection*, 1997.

Literature:

Marie Berhaut, *Caillebotte, sa vie et son œuvre, Catalogue raisonné des peintures et pastels.* Paris: Fondation Wildenstein, Bibliothèque des Arts, 1978, p. 235, no. 458, illustrated.
Kirk Varnedœ, *Gustave Caillebotte.* New Haven and London: Yale University Press, 1987, pp. 178–79, illustrated in color. (French edition published by Adam Biro, Paris, 1988).
AMFA, NY, 1987, pp. 30–31, illustrated in color.
Derek Fell, *The Impressionist Garden.* London: Frances Lincoln Ltd., 1994, p. 78, illustrated in color.
Marie Berhaut, *Caillebotte: Catalogue raisonné des peintures et pastels.* Paris: Wildenstein Institute, 1994, p. 252, illustrated in color.
AMFA, NY, 1997, pp. 56–57, no. 40, illustrated in color.

11 **Maurice Denis (1870–1943)**
La cuisinière
(The Cook)
1893

Oil on canvas
31 ½ x 23 ⅝ inches (80 x 60 cm.)
Signed with the vertical monogram and dated lower left: *MAVD 93*

Provenance:

Ambroise Vollard, 1901
Private Collection, France
Collection J.L., Cherbourg, France
[Elizabeth Royer]

Exhibitions:

Lyon, Musée des Beaux-Arts, *Maurice Denis: 1870–1943,* September 29–December 18, 1994; Köln Wallfraf–Richartz Museum, January 22–April 2, 1995: Liverpool, Walker Art Gallery, April 21–June 18, 1995; Amsterdam, Van Gogh Museum, July 7–September 17, 1995. Catalogue by Guy Cogeval, Claire Denis, and Thérèse Barruel, Ghent: Snœck-Ducaju & Zoon, 1994, pp. 188–89, no. 61, illustrated in color, illustrated on cover.
AMFA, NY, *The Whitehead Collection*, 1997.

Literature:

Ann Dumas, "Maurice Denis: Subjective States." *Art in America* April 1995: pp. 74– 75, illustrated in color.
AMFA, NY, 1997, pp. 102, 104, no. 64, illustrated in color.
To be included in the forthcoming *Catalogue raisonné de l'œuvre de Maurice Denis* in preparation by Dominique Maurice-Denis, Claire Denis, Thérèse Barruel, and Anne Gruson, Saint Germaine-en-Laye, France.

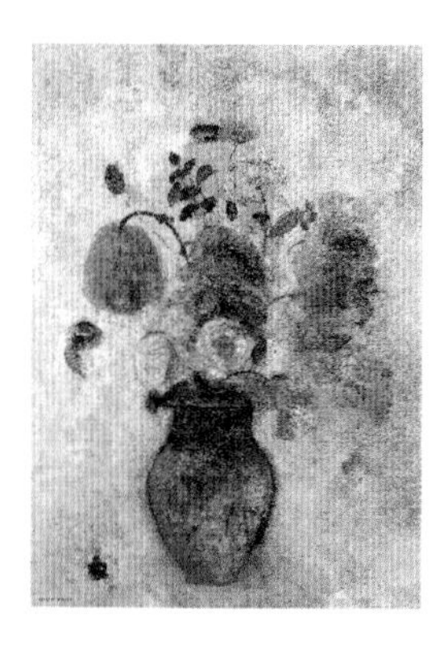

12 **Odilon Redon (1840–1916)**
Bouquet de fleurs
(Bouquet of Flowers)
circa 1912

Oil on canvas
28 ¾ x 21 ½ inches (73 x 54.6 cm.)
Signed lower left: *Odilon Redon*

Promised gift to the National Gallery of Art, Washington, D.C.

Provenance:

Marcel Kapferer, Paris (bought directly from the artist through Bernheim-Jeune, Paris)
Paul Wyler, New York, c. 1958
Wildenstein and Co., New York
Private Collection
[Forum Gallery]
[Beadleston Gallery]

Exhibitions:

Winterthur, Kunstmuseum, *Exposition d'art français,* 1917, no. 167.
Wiesbaden, Germany, 1921.
Paris, Hôtel de la Curiosité et des Beaux-Arts, *Première Exposition de collectionneurs au profit de la Société des amis du Luxembourg,* March 10–April 10, 1924, no. 124.
Paris, Musée des Arts décoratifs, *Odilon Redon, Exposition rétrospective de son œuvre,* March 1926, p. 12, no. 51.
Glasgow, Alex Reid and Lefevre, *Paintings and Pastels by Odilon Redon,* October 1926, (traveled to London, 1926, no. 2.
Paris, Musée du Petit Palais, *Odilon Redon,* 1934, p. 16, no. 47.
London, Wildenstein & Co., *Exhibition of Paintings by Odilon Redon,* 1938, no. 16.
Paris, Galerie André Weil, *Grands Maîtres dans les collections particulières, au profit de l'Orphelinat des Arts,* June 16–July 12, 1955, no. 33.
Montclair, 1989, p. 5, no. 59, illustrated. Reproduced on exhibition poster.
AMFA, NY, *The Whitehead Collection*, 1997.

Literature:

Klaus Berger, Odilon Redon: *Phantasie und Farbe.* Cologne: M. Dumont Schauberg, 1964, nos. 306, 309.
AMFA, NY, 1987, pp. 82–83, illustrated on cover.
National Gallery, 1991: Annual Report. Washington, D.C., 1992, pp. 16, 88, illustrated.
Alec Wildenstein, *Odilon Redon, catalogue raisonné de l'œuvre peint et dessiné, Vol. III, Fleurs et paysages.* Paris: Wildenstein Institute, Bibliothèque des Arts, 1996, p. 131, no. 1551, illustrated.
AMFA, NY, *The Whitehead Collection*, 1997, pp. 107–8, no. 66, illustrated in color.

13 **Auguste Rodin (1840–1917)**
Étude de femme nue
(Study of a Female Nude)
late 1890s

Pencil and reddish-brown watercolor on buff paper
12 ⅞ x 9 ¾ inches (32.7 x 24.8 cm.)
Signed lower right: *A Rodin*

Provenance:

de Hauke & Co., Inc., New York
Mrs. Douglas M. Moffatt, New York
(Christie's, New York, November 13, 1985, Lot No. 102.)

Exhibitions:

Montclair, 1989, no. 64.
AMFA, NY, *The Whitehead Collection*, 1997.

Literature:

AMFA, NY, 1987, pp. 92–93, illustrated in color.
AMFA, NY, 1997, p. 62–63, no. 43, illustrated in color.

14 **Auguste Rodin (1840–1917)**
Les Mauvais Génies
(The Evil Spirits)
1899

White marble, unique
24 x 14 ⅜ x 17 ½ inches (61 x 36.5 x 44.5 cm.)
Signed on base: *A. Rodin*

Provenance:

Galerie Georges Petit, Paris
Albert Poullot Collection, Reims
Galerie Schmit, Paris
Feingarten Galleries, Los Angeles
William Shanhouse, Iowa
[Kent Gallery]

Exhibitions:

Montclair, 1989, no. 65, illustrated on cover.
New York, 1997.
AMFA, NY, *The Whitehead Collection*, 1997.

Literature:

Georges Grappe, *Catalogue du Musée Rodin.* Paris: 1938, pl. 273, pp. 104–5.
John L. Tancock, *The Sculpture of Auguste Rodin.* Philadelphia: 1976, pp. 312–13.
AMFA, NY, 1997, pp. 64–65, no. 44, illustrated in color.

15 **Kees van Dongen (1877–1968)**
La femme à l'aigrette
(Woman with a Plume)
circa 1910

Oil on canvas
21 ¾ x 18 ¼ inches (55.2 x 46.3 cm.)
Signed upper left: *van Dongen*

Provenance:

Private Collection, Paris
[Guy Loudmer, Hôtel Drouot, Paris, November 17, 1991, Lot No. 27]

Exhibitions:

Paris, Salon d'Automne, 1911, no. 380.
Paris, Galerie Charpentier, *Cent tableaux des collections privées de Bonnard à de Staël,* 1960, illustrated.
Paris, Galerie Charpentier, *Les Fauves,* 1962, no. 129, illustrated.
Paris, Musée National d'Art Moderne, *Le Fauvisme français et les débuts de l'Expressionisme allemand,* January 15–March 6, 1966; Munich, Haus der Kunst, no. 120, illustrated.
Paris, Musée National d'Art Moderne, *Van Dongen,* October 3–November 26, 1967; Rotterdam, Musée Boymans van Beuningen, December 3, 1967–January 28, 1968, no. 78, illustrated.
AMFA, NY, *The Whitehead Collection,* 1997.

Literature:

Review of the exhibition *Cent tableaux des collections privées de Bonnard à de Staël* at Galerie Charpentier. Le Monde, April 29, 1960.
Review of the exhibition *Cent tableaux des collections privées de Bonnard à de Staël* at Galerie Charpentier. *The Burlington Magazine* 102 (June 1960): pp. 275–76, illustrated.
Les Nouvelles Littéraires, 8 March 1962, cover illustration.
Elle, 23 March 1962, p. 51, illustrated.
AMFA, NY, 1997, pp. 128–29, no. 79, illustrated in color.
To be included in the forthcoming *Catalogue raisonné de l'œuvre de Kees van Dongen* in preparation by Jacques-Chalom Des Cordes, and Christine Tolo-Froger, Wildenstein Institute, Paris.

16 **Amedeo Modigliani (1884–1920)**
Portrait de Béatrice Hastings
1916

Oil on canvas
25 9/16 x 18 1/8 inches (65 x 46 cm.)
Signed and dated upper right: *Modigliani 1916*

Provenance:

Collection Paul Guillaume, Paris
Collection Schubert, Grasse, France, 1945
[Galerie David-Garnier, 1958]
Galerie Rosengart, Lucerne, 1958
Hester Diamond, New York, 1983
[Acquavella Gallery]

Exhibitions:

Paris, Galerie Bernheim-Jeune, *La Grande peinture contemporaine dans la collection de Paul Guillaume,* May–June, 1929.
Paris, Musée d'Art Moderne de la Ville de Paris, *Amedeo Modigliani*, March 26–June 28, 1981, p. 120, no. 32, illustrated in color. (In conjunction with this exhibition, reproduced in *The Sun,* Baltimore, 14 April 1981; *Le Journal du 16e arrondissement;* Paris, April, 1981; and *La Vie Française,* Paris, 4 May 1981.)
Montclair, 1989, no. 47.
AMFA, NY, *The Whitehead Collection*, 1997.
New York, The Jewish Museum, *Paris in New York: French Artists in Private Collections,* March 5–June 25, 2000, Catalogue edited by Susan Chevlowe with an essay by Romy Golan, p. 48, no. 29, illustrated in color, reproduced on exhibition poster.
Buffalo, Albright Knox Art Gallery, *Modigliani and the Artists of Montparnasse,* October 18, 2002–January 12, 2003; Fort Worth, Texas, Kimbell Art Museum, February 8–May 25, 2003; Los Angeles, Los Angeles County Museum of Art, June 28–September 28, 2003.

Literature:

George Waldemar, *Modigliani, l'amour de l'art.* Paris, October 1925, p. 384, no. 1, illustrated as *Portrait de fillette.*
Georges Michel, *Les Montparnos.* Paris: Fasquelle Editeurs, 1929, p. 251, illustrated.
Arthur Pfannstiel, *Modigliani.* Paris: Editions Marcel Seheur, 1929, pp. 10, 22, illustrated.
George Waldemar, *La Grande peinture contemporaine dans la collection de Paul Guillaume.* Paris: Galerie Bernheim-Jeune, 1929, p. 144.
Carl Einstein, *Die Kunst des 20. Jahrhunderts.* Berlin, 1926, p. 224, illustrated.
Carl Einstein, *Die Kunst des 20. Jahrhunderts.* Berlin, 1931, pp. 231, 294, illustrated.
Nietta Aprà, *Tormento di Modigliani.* Milan: Casa Editrice Bietti, 1945, p. 113, illustrated.
Gotthard Jedlicka, *Modigliani.* Erlenbach-Zürich: Eugen Rentsch Verlag, 1953, p. 82, pl. 14, illustrated.
Giovanni di San Lazzaro, *Modigliani Peintures.* Paris: Les Editions du Chêne, 1953, p. 5, no. 12, illustrated.
Jacques Lipchitz, *Amedeo Modigliani.* New York: Harry N. Abrams, Inc., 1954, pl. 19, illustrated.
Arthur Pfannstiel, *Modigliani et son œuvre.* Paris: Etude critique et catalogue raisonné, Bibliothèque des Arts, 1956, p. 76, no. 69, illustrated.
Ambrogio Ceroni, *Amedeo Modigliani, Peintre.* Milan: Edizioni del Milione, 1958, p. 50, no. 57.
Ambrogio Ceroni and Leone Piccioni, *Das gemalte Werk von Modigliani.* Milan: Editione Rizzoli, 1970, no. 109.
Joseph Lanthemann, *Modigliani, Catalogue raisonné.* Barcelona, 1970, no. 32.
Leone Piccioni and Ambrogio Ceroni, *I dipinti di Modigliani.* Milan: Rizzoli Editore, 1972, p. 93, no. 109, illustrated.
Jacques Lassaigne, *Amedeo Modigliani, Werkverzeichnis.* Frankfurt: Ullstein Kunst-Buch 1981, p. 32, no. 9, illustrated.
AMFA, NY, 1987, pp. 62–63, illustrated in color.
Christian Parisot, *Modigliani catalogue raisonné, Peintures, dessins, aquarelles.* Vol. 2. Livorno: Editions Graphis Arte, 1991, pp. 110, 292, illustrated.
Anette Kruszynski, *Amedeo Modigliani, Akte und Porträts.* Munich-New York: Prestel-Verlag, 1996, p. 57, illustrated in color.
AMFA, NY, 1997, pp. 140-42, no. 85, illustrated in color.
Achim Moeller, *In Good Hands: 25 Years of Art in the Life of a Dealer.* New York: Achim Moeller Fine Art, 1997, pp. 32–33, 76–77.

17 **Pablo Ruiz Picasso (1881–1973)**
Ragtime—Two Musicians,
for Igor Stravinsky (recto)
Three Musicians (verso)
Projet pour la couverture
de la partition de "Ragtime"
d'Igor Stravinsky
(Design for the Cover
of the Score of Igor Stravinsky's
"Ragtime")
1918–19

Pen and ink on paper
10 ¾ x 7 ¼ inches (26 x 18.5 cm.)
Signed lower right: *Picasso*

Provenance:
Achim Moeller, London, 1973
Martin Ackerman (Sotheby's, New York, May 11, 1988, Lot No. 121)

Exhibitions:
London, Achim Moeller, *Selected Paintings, Drawings and Graphics of the 19th and 20th Centuries,* 1973, illustrated p. 7.
Montclair, 1989, p. 23, no. 54, illustrated.
AMFA, NY, *The Whitehead Collection*, 1997.

Literature:
Christian Zervos, *Pablo Picasso, Volume 6, Supplément aux Volumes 1 à 5.* Paris, 1954, p. 160, no. 1344, illustration of sheet music cover. (Zervos illustrates the sheet music cover rather than the drawing, which he evidently had not seen, since he notes neither the medium nor the size in his description).
John Russell, "At Cézanne's Elbow." *Sunday Times,* London, 18 November 1973.
Arts Review (February 1974).
Picasso's Paintings, Watercolors, Drawings and Sculpture. A Comprehensive Illustrated Catalogue 1885–1973: From Cubism to Neoclassicism 1917–1919. San Francisco: Alan Wofsy, 1995, p. 284, no. 19-369, illustrated.
cf. Sotheby's, New York, November 12, 1996, Lot No. 29. Catalogue entry for Pablo Picasso, *Portrait of Igor Stravinsky,* 1920.
AMFA, NY, 1997, pp. 166–67, no. 97, illustrated in color.

18 **Georges Braque (1882–1963)**
Tête de femme II
(Head of a Woman II)
also Profils (Profiles)
1930

Oil on canvas
18 x 15 inches (45.7 x 38.1 cm.)
Signed and dated lower right: *G Braque 30*

Provenance:

Mr. and Mrs. Walter Bareiss, Greenwich, Conn.
[Sotheby's, New York, April 27, 1960, sale for the benefit of The Museum of Modern Art, Lot No. 32]
Paul Rosenberg and Company, New York
Nathan Cummings, New York
[Artcurial]

Exhibitions:

Washington, D.C., National Gallery of Art, *Selections from the Nathan Cummings Collection,* June 28–September 11, 1970; New York, The Metropolitan Museum of Art, July 1–September 7, 1971. Catalogue with introduction by Douglas Cooper, 1970, p. 63, no. 48, illustrated.
Chicago, The Art Institute of Chicago, *Major Works from the Collection of Nathan Cummings,* October 20–December 9, 1973, p. 52, no. 43.
Montclair, 1989, no. 9.
AMFA, NY, *The Whitehead Collection*, 1997.

Literature:

"Georges Braque." *Cahiers d'Art* 8 (1933), p. 78, illustrated.
Carl Einstein, "Georges Braque, XXe Siècle." *Chroniques du Jour,* Paris 1934, pl. LXXXII.
Maurice Gieure, *G. Braque*. Paris: Editions Pierre Tisné, 1956, p. 19, illustrated.
Catalogue de l'œuvre de Georges Braque, peintures 1928–1935. Paris: Maeght Editeur, 1962, pp. 39–40, illustrated.
AMFA, NY, 1987, pp. 28–29, illustrated in color.
AMFA, NY, 1997, pp. 162–64, no. 95, illustrated in color.

19 **Henri Matisse (1869–1954)**
Tête de jeune fille
(Head of a Girl)
1949

Charcoal on laid paper
16 x 12 inches (40.7 x 30.7 cm.)
Signed and dated lower right: *H. Matisse 49*

Provenance:
Curt Valentin Gallery, New York
Feigl Gallery, New York
Hans and Maria Lehfeldt, New York

Exhibitions:
New York, Curt Valentin Gallery, *The Sculpture of Henri Matisse,* February 10–28, 1953, p. 14, no. 59, illustrated.
AMFA, NY, *The Whitehead Collection*, 1997.

Literature:
AMFA, NY, 1997, p. 136–37, no. 83, illustrated in color.

20 **Henri Matisse (1869–1954)**
Nature Morte, Pêches et Verre
(Still Life, Peaches and Glass)
circa 1918

Oil on canvas
8 ⅞ x 10 ⅞ inches (22.5 x 27.7 cm.)
Signed lower left: *Henri Matisse*
Painted in Issy-les-Moulineaux

Provenance:

M. Parent, Paris
Galerie Bernheim-Jeune, Paris, 1925
Carstairs Gallery, New York, 1926
M. Knoedler & Co., New York, 1927
M. Frick, New York
Sacha Guitry, Paris, as of 1931
Galerie Pétridès, Paris
Stephen Hahn, New York
Martha Baer, New York
(Sotheby's, New York, November 12, 1999, Lot. No. 0289.)

Exhibitions:

New York, M. Knoedler & Co., *Exhibition of French Art of the Last Fifty Years,* 1927.
Paris, Galerie Georges Petit, *Henri Matisse,* 1931, no. 41.
Washington, D.C., National Gallery of Art, *Henri Matisse: The Early Years in Nice, 1916–1930,* November 2, 1986–March 29, 1987, no. 42.

Literature:

Albert Barnes and Violette de Mazia, *The Art of Henri Matisse.* New York and London: C. Scribner's sons, 1933, p. 44, illustrated.
Sacha Guitry, *Cent Merveilles.* Paris: R. Solar, 1954, p. 131, illustrated.
Jack Cowart and Dominique Fourcade, *Henri Matisse: The Early Years in Nice, 1916–1930.* Washington, D.C. and New York: National Gallery of Art and Harry N. Abrams, 1986.
Guy Patrice and Michel Dauberville, *Matisse: Henri Matisse chez Bernheim-Jeune.* Vol. 1. Paris: Bernheim-Jeune, 1995, p. 629, no. 212, illustrated.

Abbreviations

AMFA, NY, *The Whitehead Collection*, 1997.
New York, Achim Moeller Fine Art, *The Whitehead Collection: Late 19th and 20th Century French Masters,* April 15–May 17, 1997. Catalogue with forewords by John C. Whitehead and Achim Moeller and an introduction by Charles F. Stuckey.

AMFA, NY, 1997
The Whitehead Collection: Late 19th and 20th Century French Masters. New York: Achim Moeller Fine Art, 1997, with forewords by John C. Whitehead and Achim Moeller and an introduction by Charles F. Stuckey.

Montclair, 1989, no.
Montclair, N.J., The Montclair Art Museum, *Late XIX and Early XX Century French Masters: The John C. Whitehead Collection,* April 30–June 18, 1989. Catalogue with a preface by Robert J. Koening and forewords by John C. Whitehead and Achim Moeller and an introduction by Charles F. Stuckey.

AMFA, NY, 1987
Late XIX and Early XX Century French Masters: The John C. Whitehead Collection. New York: Achim Moeller Fine Art, 1987, with forewords by John C. Whitehead and Achim Moeller and an introduction by Charles F. Stuckey.

English translations of French titles, where they are not specified in the literature, are those of the editors.

Acknowledgements

I am grateful to J. Carter Brown, Director Emeritus of the National Gallery of Art, for his brilliant tribute to John C. Whitehead in this publication. My warm thanks also go to Charles F. Stuckey, who gave much knowledgeable help and advice throughout this project and who has written an enlightening introduction to the collection.

I am indebted to the scholars who generously answered our questions. In particular I thank Colin B. Bailey, Chief Curator of the Frick Collection, and Michael Pantazzi, Associate Curator of European and American Art at the National Gallery of Canada, for sharing their extraordinary knowledge of Renoir and Daumier respectively.

Warmest thanks are due those who worked on the production of this catalogue: Philippe Apeloig for his handsome design; Laura Kleger for her careful editing; Paola Gribaudo for her exceptional coordination and printing skills; Giancarlo Zampollo, and his staff at Litho Art New, for lending his fine understanding of color to the project; Janet Cavallero for her meticulous research; and Noel Allum for his excellent photographs.

Denise Emmett in John C. Whitehead's office gave much assistance with gracious patience. Nicholas D'Avella, Ute Proellochs, and particularly Branwen Buckley of the gallery, and my extraordinary wife Colette also helped to make both the exhibition and the catalogue a success.

Achim Moeller

March 2002

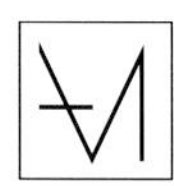

Achim Moeller Fine Art, Ltd.
167 East 73rd Street,
New York, NY 10021

T. (212) 988-4500
F. (212) 988-5400
info@moellerart.com
www.moellerart.com

Thirtieth Anniversary
(Founded London 1972–
New York 1984)

Member of the Art Dealers
Association of America
and the Syndicat National
des Antiquaires
Négociants en Objets d'Art,
Tableaux Anciens et Modernes,
France